In and Out
of the
Shadows

In and Out of the Shadows

David Selby

Locust GROVE

In and Out of the Shadows
David Selby

ISBN: 0-9701282-1-5
Second Printing 2000
For information, contact www.davidselby.com
Cover Photographs: Erik Heinila (front portrait);
Holly Cobert (front inset); Mark Sennet (back cover)

Project Coordinator: Jim Pierson
Book & Cover Design: Cheryl Carrington

Poetry © 1999 David Selby

Photographs & Artwork Courtesy: ABC-TV, Associated Film Distribution,
Barter Theater, CBS-TV, Cinerama Releasing, Cleveland Playhouse, Dan Curtis
Productions, Walt Disney Productions, T. Charles Erickson, Friedman-Abeles,
Harmony Gold, Al Hirschfeld, Ellen Jaskol, Liz Kaul, Dee Kearney, Lorimar,
MGM/UA, Walter Miller Jr., Cliff Moore, NBC-TV, Jay Nass, Barry Null, *Playbill*,
Rysher Entertainment, The Shakespeare Theatre, *16 Magazine*, Sullivan
Productions, Turner Entertainment, Twentieth Century-Fox, Warner Brothers

For Chip, J.T., Brooke and Amanda

and
Ed Limato.

With love and gratitude.

There were always *Dark Shadows* fans waiting to greet the cast outside the studio.

Note the graffiti on the picture at the lower left—"I hate Bob. We *all* hate Bob!" Bob was the security guard who kept the fans at bay.

Acknowledgments

Nancy Barrett, Dave Brown, Beatrice Donnelly,
Mary Donnelly, Robert Finocchio, Charles Randolph Greane,
Norma Keller, LA Theatre Works, Mary Lesher, Ben Martin,
Geoff Miller, Pepper Pierson, Kathleen Resch, Marcy Robin,
Kathryn Leigh Scott, Susan Sullivan, Jeff Thompson,
Ann Wilson and the entire Selby family.

Foreword

The poet Robert Frost wrote about a solitary traveler in one of my favorite poems. The traveler had to decide which road to take at a juncture in his life. He took the less traveled road, which made all the difference, according to the poet. I feel a real affinity with that unknown man who stood at a crossroads. He did not take the expected route.

How did a young man from the mountains of West Virginia end up in the acting business? Going to live plays or any kind of concerts were not part of my growing-up years. I read comic books, rode my bike, and played baseball. Where then the urge, the undeniable drive to leave my beloved hills and strike out on my own? The mystery is there in each of us. How we respond is what sets us off on a particular path.

This photo-journey book is an acknowledgment of appreciation to all of the people over the years who have enjoyed my work and supported my career, beginning with those days in New York on 53rd Street where the television series *Dark Shadows* was filmed. I feel blessed to have been able to pursue my life's dream. But, most importantly, I have never been a solitary traveler.

David Selby

Contents

THE ROAD OF HAPPENSTANCE

The course of a life is a road of happenstance

So this road has no destination
like a burr riding on the pantsleg
you are dropped and left to sprout
with no knowledge of where you came
or where you are to go—a drifter
and like an orphan you are lonely
no matter how deep you prospect for answers
But time passes like in an old book store
And somehow you grow enlarged
from a child's wants that were lost
and cannot be returned

With lips to play the trombone
you cannot be a drummer boy
Or walk the queen down the isle
if you are an awkward boy
but you stumble into acting
because you look like you could
and be ordained a minister
because you sound like you could
Just a wanderer picking at life
like a hungry man in a trash can
knowing there is no going back
either riding on or getting off
so you cast the dice
because the road does not stop
it only bids farewell

Beginnings

CHILD OF THE FIFTIES

A child of the fifties
A hill child
A seed of mountain men and women
(and there were women)
An all-American boy
if I dare
Square and good
Optimistic and pleasant
Eager to please
A soldier
Simple like the fifties
and as bland as a pile of dirt
The Depression was not my memory
Nor hardly the great war
I knew what was good
and what was bad
Black and white
Like those *Life* photographs
I remember my first suit
(yes it was gray flannel)
as careful as my
crewcut was easy
our first refrigerater
first washing machine
first car
first record player
first record
(Bill Haley's "Rock Around The Clock")
I would marry well
be financially secure
live happily everafter
then theatre found me

I didn't know any misfits
or rejects or criminals
homosexuals or other deviants
but now I got to read about them
and meet a few
and none of them spelled theater with an "re"
I liked that
I discovered a temper
as wicked as lightening
and depression
my own little gray cloud
but my parents weren't the enemies
and I couldn't spell alienation
So go figure
Like the fifties
the pot was brewing
It never was black and white
Maybe because I was so damned ignorant
even now
incompleteness
I must be getting old
But I am still married
and thanks to the fifties
that is one thing I did well
and dear children
you are the gifts
to prove it

With his grandmother.

With parents, Clyde and Sarah Selby

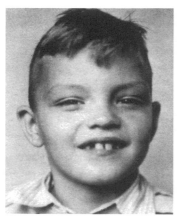

With Smiley Burnette.

Top left with Buck
and Taffy.

With brother Craig,
left and top right.

Top left: With his wife, Chip, in college.
Bottom: With Chip, a few years later.
Next page: Eddie, Walt, David and Butch.

MUTINEERS

Butch, Eddie, and Walt, and I
Four mutineers of long ago
One hot summer day on the block
watching puffballs blow
saw old man Shank paving his walk
We hid behind the maple tree
conspiring our immortality
Laughing at the chance to sow
we commandeered the paver's woe
with handprints four in a row

Butch, Eddie, and Walt, and I
Four mutineers of long ago
had no idea where puffballs go
That's for Mother Wind to know

Butch in Pittsburg, six children in tow
Eddie in D.C., a judge I hear
Walt, a teacher, and every penny dear
And I in yet another show

Planted seeds to weed and hoe
the wishes of each we hope will grow
only to scatter to and fro

But four little handprints greet each dawn
fossilized, our Parthenon
Open palms of innocence bond

And I can never let it go
Four mutineers of long ago

9

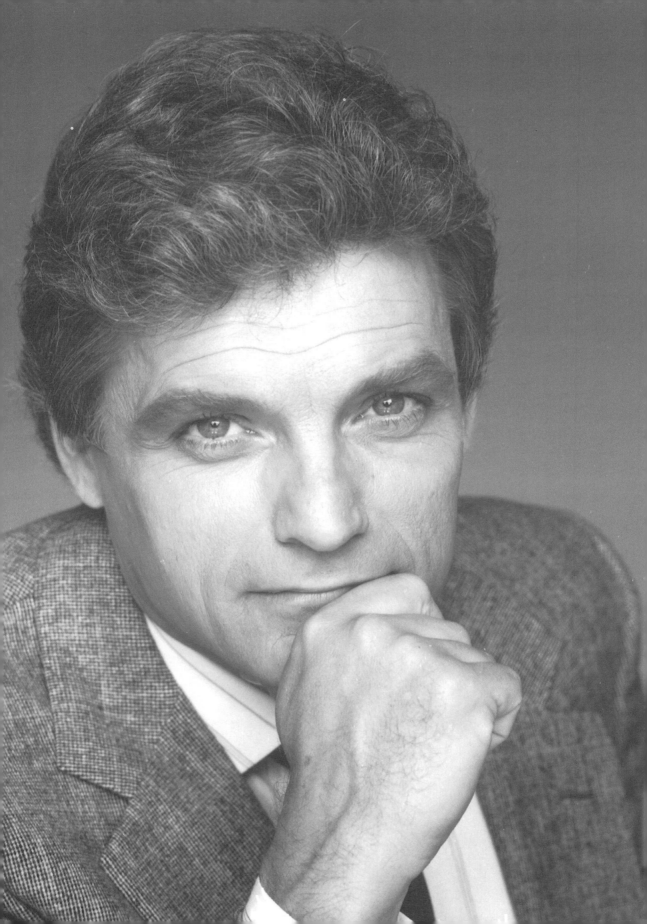

THE HEAD SHOT

The bane of an actor's life
besides unemployment?
The "head shot"
on which no two people ever agree
Nice eyes
droopy lids
full lips
mouth's immense
sweet smile
a little forced
That eight by ten
decorating the walls of car washes
body shops, delis, hardware stores
and bad restaurants
There's the no money, clueless,
straight out of the yearbook headshot
The no money no hassle taken by a friend headshot
The hard-earned first professional
old chin on your hand headshot
The glamour ala Tab Hunter headshot
The I don't give a damn take me as I am headshot
The real, cool, suave, sophisticated, stern, sexy, sweet, pouty,
sensitive, penetrating please God
get me a job
too bad it doesn't look like you headshot
You scrimp and save
Pay another "hot" photographer
who shoots "individuals"
who knows what "they" are looking for
who gets the best out of you
sees your best side
Then go blind looking at proof sheets
agonizing desperately searching
for the one vital, mysterious, wonderfully gorgeous shot
that doesn't exist except with Cary Grant
showing warmth, softness and charming accessiblity
under a layer of streetwise toughness
with a coat of dignity and a liner of integrity.
Everything and nothing.
Can they see the heart in those eyes
whose teared blood runs down the hands
that blithely toss another anonymous fragile face
splintered glass, shredded bits and pieces
in the bottom of the trash can
Faces, whose only crime is to aspire,
that want to reach up
and grab that second assistant's assistant
by the neck forcing a second look
at what that face is made of.

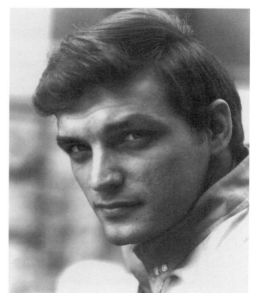

Dark Shadows

Thirty some years ago, so far away
But the memories through time do burn
as if they happened only yesterday
and back to Collinwood I do return

When a certain evil ghost did appear
with a spell to cast and a plot to scheme
Luring children to a room so to hear
an old gramophone playing Quentin's theme

His frock coat covered a physique so lean
you knew he had something mean up his sleave
All his wickedness had yet to be seen
His spirit was such they had to believe

There was no choice but to pack up and leave
But Barnabas came to even the score
Though ended back where he couldn't forsee
Trapped in his coffin, a vampire once more

He travels through time where Quentin's alive
Mysteries, secrets, and intrigues galore
and son-of-a-gun the ratings revive
with millions of fans clamoring for more

Dark Shadows had more surprises of doom
Quentin's a zombie who rises and walks
Then is a werewolf who howls at full moon
But in day sounds normal now that he talks

Suddenly a cure for his curse is found
Which Count Petofi finally effects
Now Quentin's immortal and more renowned
But the vampire's taste for beautiful necks

again wrecks havoc with Barnabas' life
When Angélique dies, Barnabas is lost
So is his chance for a beautiful wife
Grief-stricken he knows what all this has cost

And with Julia, climbs the staircase through time
Then Quentin destroys the stairs to the past
But the memories are there, yours and mine
Shadows of the night and the spell they cast

Judith (Joan Bennett) gives Quentin a piece of her mind.

Barnabas (Jonathan Frid) and Quentin in a
typically dramatic moment at Collinwood.

Reading lines with
Jonathan Frid.

Rehearsing
with Jonathan.

Sharing a laugh with director
Henry Kaplan and Denise
Nickerson; giving instructions
to wardrobe mistress June Puleo,
while Mike Stroka looks on.

Shadows Of The Night

("Quentin's Theme" from "Dark Shadows")

Words by
CHARLES GREAN

Music by
ROBERT COBER

JUDITH: "That music will drive me mad!"

Quentin struggles to reach his grave.

Rehearsing with Roger Davis; taping with
Denise Nickerson and Thayer David.

Chris Pennock, Lara Parker, Denise Nickerson and Selby run through the script with director Henry Kaplan and production assistant Harriet Rohr.

A close shave before the show.

Selby's *16* Magazine "teen idol" pose.

Quentin has his own trading cards, just like the baseball players.

Evan Hanley (Humbert Allen Astredo) and Quentin.

Maggie (Kathryn Leigh Scott) and Quentin steal a kiss.

A shoot for *Tiger Beat* magazine.

Rehearsing with
Grayson Hall

Watson and Sherlock Holmes?
No—it's Count Petofi and Quentin.

Barnabas (Jonathan Frid) questions Jamison (David Henesy) as Quentin looks on.

Vincent Loscalzo
gives David the
Dark Shadows look.

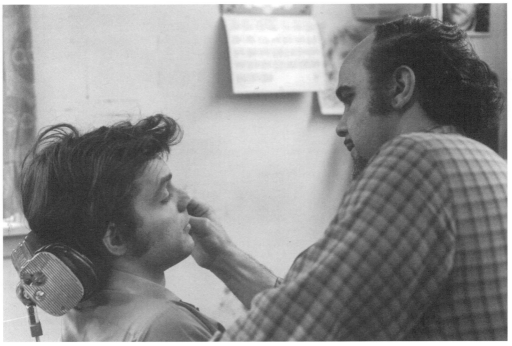

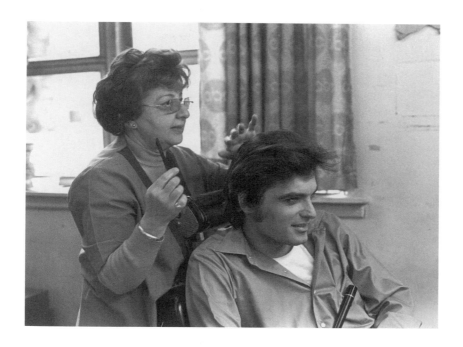

Hair stylist Edith Tilles coifs Selby to perfection;
An interview for *Tiger Beat* magazine.

Reverend Gregory Trask (Jerry Lacy) attempts
to exorcise Quentin from a zombie state.

Facing page: Selby and Nancy Barrett recorded *I Wanna Dance With You*, which
was featured on an episode of *Dark Shadows* and was issued as a single record.

Rehearsing with
Lara Parker, Chris
Pennock, and
Michael Stroka.

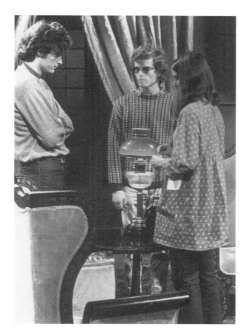

Working on a scene (left)
with Jim Storm and Kate
Jackson; pondering a
mysterious note (below).

Studying script
and relaxing.

The typical actor admiring himself.

Selby's appearance at the "I Am An American" parade in Baltimore
in 1969 brought out a rash of *Dark Shadows* fans.

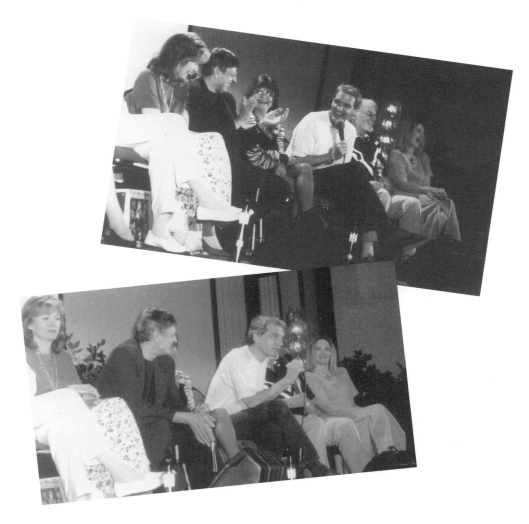

Reuniting with *DS* castmates Kathryn Leigh Scott, Michael Stroka,
Denise Nickerson, Dennis Patrick and Lara Parker at the
1996 *Dark Shadows* Festival in Los Angeles.

Stage

TEACHER

Thought stern as an old testament preacher
this lonely but oddly friendly creature
in such a dangerous occupation
but as much fun as a double feature
is how I remember my tenth grade teacher

Who despite my procrastination
would force feed my imagination
with a patience only she would engage
You've no talent for accumulation
was her startling revelation

So you may as well prepare for the stage
at least enjoy your very meager wage
and that joy will be your salvation
offered my kindly precisely sage
You will spread my seed across the age

if you follow my recommendation
I did and will for her celebration
of her loving caring dedication
where every role I feel her elation
and always hear her standing ovation

"He that troubleth his own house
Shall inherit the wind."
Proverbs: 11:29

INHERIT THE WIND   August 11-15, 1965

With Michael Flanagan in a summer stock
production of *Inherit the Wind*.

Opposite page: Selby as Prince Hal in
Henry the IV with George Hearn as Hotspur
at the Goodman Theatre in Chicago.

Portraying the young
Abe Lincoln in
Prologue to Glory.

Top left and above: As Rev. Batelle, Selby preaches in the historical drama
Honey in the Rock, an outdoor presentation in West Virginia.

As Valentine in Shaw's *You Never Can Tell.*

Krapps' Last Tape.

Selby is the spear carrier on the far left in the
Barter Theatre production of *Twelfth Night*.

Recognize Selby? He's the bear in this Saroyan
production of *The Time of Your Life* at the Barter.

Selby as King Alonso in Shakespeare's *The Tempest*,
at the Cleveland Playhouse, with Keith Mackey.

Starring as Abe Lincoln in *Mr. Highpockets*
(with Richard Bergman as the Devil), and in *U.S.A.*
(with Jeanne Vanderbilt and Marjorie Johnson).

Selby played Richard Merrick in the national touring company of
The Impossible Years, pictured here with Sam Levene, Madeleine Fisher
and Elizabeth Fleming (above); as Doug Hall in *Yes, My Darling Daughter*
with Alice Arlen at the Equity Library Theatre (below left).

Right: Selby and Madeleine Fisher
in *The Impossible Years*.

PLAYBILL

QUEENS THEATRE-IN-THE-PARK

THE PLAYBOY OF THE
WESTERN WORLD

By
John Millington Synge

Queens Theatre in the Park
Playwrights
Horizons

With Kaiulani Lee in
*Playboy of the Western
World*, off-Broadway.

Left: As David in Joseph Papp's
production of David Rabe's
Sticks and Bones.

Below: As Cisco, off-Broadway, in
Sam Shepard's *The Unseen Hand*.

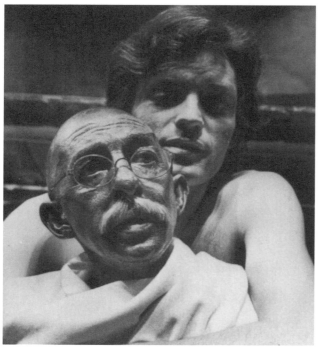

In *Gandhi* with
Jack McGowan,
Selby as the Antagonist.

As Dick Dudgeon in
The Devil's Disciple at
the American Shakespeare
Festival in Stratford,
Connecticut with
Jill Clayburgh.

Siamese Connections (left to right): William Hickey, Selby
(as Franklin Kroner, Jr.), Catherine Damon, Roberts Blossom,
James Staley and Ralph Roberts.

At the Arlington Park Theatre in Chicago, Selby
was Clym Yeobeight in *Dance on a Country Grave*.
Above left: Avril Gentles, Selby and Indira Danks;
and right: Selby and Gentles.

Selby with Laura
Henry, Marcia
Winkelmann and
Patrick Henry.

Echoes: Selby as Sam with Lynn Milgrim on Broadway.

Selby was Doc in *The Family* with Dale Soules and
Brent Spiner, a Chelsea Theatre off-Broadway production.

A treasured Hirshfeld drawing for the *New York Times* of *Eccentricities of a Nightingale*. Left to right: Shepperd Strudwick, Nan Martin, Betsy Palmer and Selby.

Below: Selby with Betsy Palmer.

John woos Jane Alexander
in *The Heiress*.

The Heiress with Jan Miner.

A pair of scenes from *Toys In The Attic* at the McCarter Theatre; In *Rib Cage*, Selby played Hodge. Other cast members include Alley Mills, John Strasberg, Ellen Endicott and Janet Ward.

As Dave Krelack in *A Hundred Percent Alive* at the Westwood Playhouse
with John Strasberg and Sabra Jones.

Selby was Dom in *I Won't
Dance* on Broadway, with
Arlene Golonka (left) and
Shirley Knight (above).

With Geraldine Page in *A Woman of Paris*.

Backstage and bearded
for *Hedda Gabler* at the
Huntington Theatre in Boston
and the Stamford Theatre in
Stamford, Connecticut.

The *Hedda Gabler* troupe.

Selby as John Proctor in *The Crucible* at L.A. Theatre Center,
with Heather Graham, Philip Baker Hall and Ann Gee Byrd
in the foreground from left.

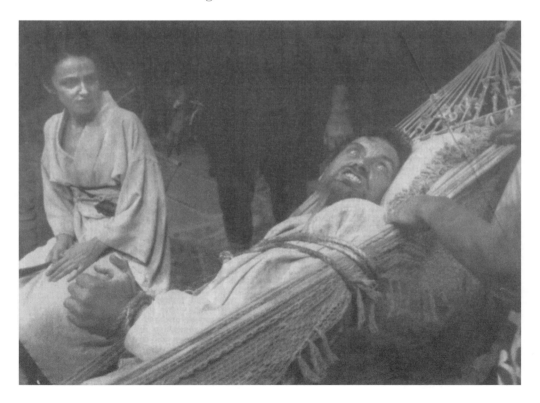

Pamela Gien as Hannah Jelkes opposite Selby as Reverend Shannon
in L.A. Theatre Center's *Night of the Iguana*.

Selby's Benedick to Kelly McGillis'
Beatrice in *Much Ado About
Nothing* at Washington D.C.'s
Shakespeare Theatre, directed
by Michael Kahn.

The American premiere of *Money & Friends*, directed by Michael Blakemore, in Los Angeles with John McMartin and John Getz.

Above: Backstage with fellow cast members from *Much Ado About Nothing*—
Selby, Jack Ryland, Edward Gero and Emery Battis.

Left to right: Sareen Mitchell, Dina Spybey, Selby, Betty Buckley, Peter Maloney and Josh Hamilton in *The Perfectionist*. Directed by Emily Mann at the McCarter Theatre in Princeton, New Jersey.

In *Lincoln and James* (written by Selby): Charles Turner, Selby and Horace-Alexander Young.

Selby on stage as Tyrone
and Ellen Burstyn as Mary, in
Eugene O'Neill's *Long Day's
Journey Into Night*.

Ian Kahn, Ellen Burstyn
and Rick Stear.

Long Day's Journey Into Night

Film

TREE OF LIFE

Saw your play
Dark character
Not what I'm looking for
then why am i here
I start to leave
Let me take a polaroid
Sure
He takes twelve
Points to one and says
That's Paul
I see—do I?
I want you to audition
Sure
On tape
Sure

They liked your audition
Great
Want you to fly to L. A.
Sure
Meet the star
Sure

She talked alot
about a tree
in her yard
It was reported
I didn't talk
much
Why?

I don't know much about trees
I saw a hole in my sweater
I put my hand over it
Thought of my mother
I should have apologized
For not talking?

For the hole I
I
You got the role
Jesus
I better read up on trees

I did
I love my trees
Come on over
I won't look the other way
holes in my sweater don't matter
You shall see a face
Read what you will
It is a place where the dog can bark
and you can put your feet up
and look at the trees

Jason Robards and Selby sharing a laugh
during filming of *Raise the Titanic*.

Opposite page: *Night of Dark Shadows*.

John Karlen played Selby's best friend, writer Alex Jenkins.

In *Night Of Dark Shadows*, Selby played dual roles of Quentin (pictured here) and Charles Collins. Grayson Hall played Carlotta Drake, the mysterious housekeeper, and Kate Jackson played his bride Tracy.

Above: A rare moment
of calm with John
Karlen, Nancy Barrett
and Kate Jackson.

Angélique (Lara Parker) seduces Charles.

A tender moment with Quentin and Tracy.

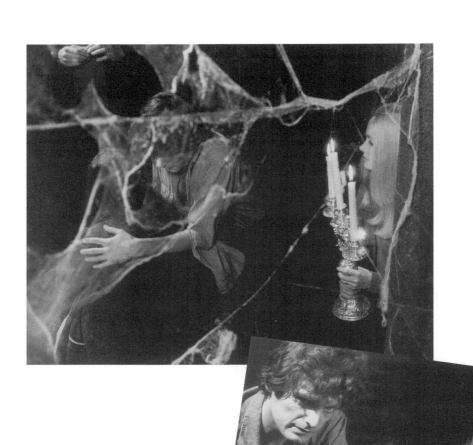

Quentin and Claire
(Nancy Barrett) comfort
a terrified Tracy.

Searching the spooky
basement at Collinwood.

Charles Collins, Reverend Strack (Thayer David) and Gabriel Collins
(Chris Pennock) view Angélique's hanging.

A pensive moment in the Collinwood stables.

With Barbra Streisand in *Up The Sandbox*.

A family outing in *Up The Sandbox*

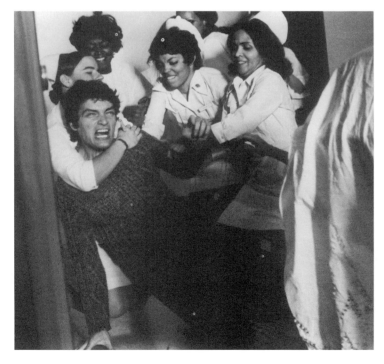

A dream
sequence from
Up the Sandbox.

Selby played Scott and Maud Adams was Paula in *The Girl In Blue*, a Canadian film, also released as *U-Turn*.

Interrogating a young girl (Christiane Robinson) about the identity of *The Girl In Blue*. Gay Rowan is Bonnie, the estranged girlfriend.

Super Cops: based on a true-life Brooklyn police duo nicknamed
"Batman and Robin." Selby was Robin (Bobby Hantz).

Above: Ron Leibman was Selby's *Super Cops* co-star.
Below: Making an arrest.

More *Super Cop*s: Selby is decorated by Pat Hingle.

Above: In *Rich Kids*, Selby was Steve Sloan, lawyer and lover to Madeline Philips, played by Kathryn Walker. Below: The *Rich Kids* cast included, left to right: John Lithgow, Kathryn Walker, Terry Kiser, Dianne Kirksy, Selby, Paul Dooley and Roberta Maxwell.

Left and above: In *Raise The Titanic*: Selby played a scientist involved with a government project to raise the infamous sunken ship.

Raise The Titanic:
Selby and Richard Jordan—
above and below at a graveyard
in Cornwall.

Selby with
Richard Jordan.

A reflective moment
with Anne Archer.

In *Rich And Famous*, Selby, as Doug Blake, was married to Candice Bergen (right) and in love with her best friend, Jacqueline Bisset (next page).

In *Dying Young*, Selby was the father of a terminally ill son.
He played in *Intersection* with Richard Gere.

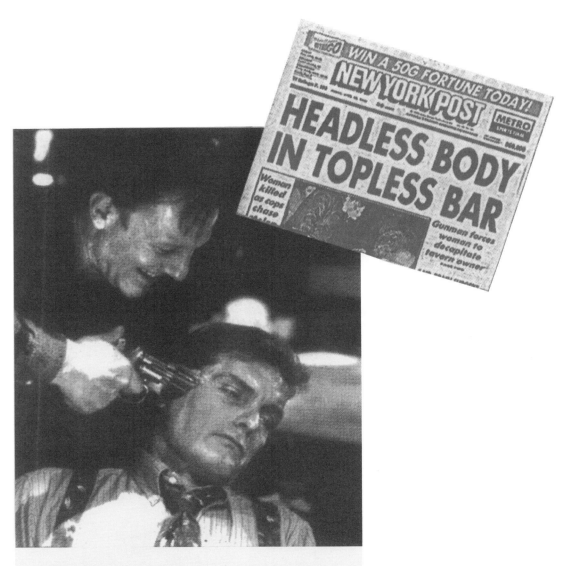

Selby as Bradford Lumkin picks the wrong night to
go to the Baby Doll Lounge. He is held hostage by
Raymond J. Barry in *Headless Body in a Topless Bar*.

Selby was an overbearing father in *White Squall* and is
pictured here with Jill Larson, who played his wife.

In *Mighty Ducks 3*, Selby portrayed
the idiosyncratic principal.

Television

GONNA SIT AND WATCH THE SEASONS ROLL BY

It's a tangled up day
when I hear myself say
gonna sit and watch the seasons roll by
gonna pack up my gear
forget a thing called career
gonna sit and watch the seasons roll by
take a permanent recess
from the chain of success
gonna sit and watch the seasons roll by
forget yesterday's sorrow
the disasters of tomorrow
gonna sit and watch the seasons roll by

It's a tangled up day
when I hear myself say
gonna sit and watch the seasons roll by
gonna cross that line
to a gentler kind
where the nights fall easy on my mind
gonna sit and watch the seasons roll by
though you're saying I couldn't if I tried
but with you by my side
we'd have a wonderful ride
watching the seasons go rolling by

It's a tangled up day
when I hear myself say
gonna sit and watch the seasons roll by
so I look to the day
when I truly can say
gonna sit and watch the seasons roll by
here they'll find me on my time to die

Flamingo Road: Michael Tyrone and Lute-Mae Sanders (Stella Stevens).

Flamingo Road cast, 1981-82.
Top left, clockwise: Selby, Morgan Fairchild, Barbara Rush, Cristina Raines,
Stella Stevens, John Beck, Glenn Robards, Kevin McCarthy, Woody Brown,
Mark Harmon, Gina Gallego, Peter Donat, Fernando Allende and Howard Duff.

Flamingo Road with John Beck (Sam Curtis) and
Howard Duff (Sheriff Titus Semple).

Flamingo Road behind the scenes with Stella Stevens and Morgan Fairchild.

Falcon Crest Cast, 1982-83 season.
Seated: Jane Wyman. First Row, left to right: Robert Foxworth,
Jamie Rose, Ana-Alicia, Susan Sullivan, Chou-Li Chi. Second Row, left
to right: William R. Moses, Abby Dalton, Lorenzo Lamas, Margaret Ladd.
Top Row, left to right: Mel Ferrer, Shannon Tweed, Selby.

Jane Wyman was *Falcon Crest* matriarch Angela Channing.

Falcon Crest:
Richard and Maggie
(Susan Sullivan).

The marriage of Richard and Maggie.

Behind the scenes.

Rehearsing on location with Ana-Alicia (Melissa), Susan Sullivan (Maggie), Margaret Ladd (Emma) and Jane Wyman (Angela).

With Shannon Tweed.

With Jane and Lorenzo.

Leslie Caron and Gina
Lollabrigida were both
guest stars on *Falcon Crest*
for a limited time.

Kim Novak (above) spent a season on *Falcon Crest* as the mysterious Kit Marlowe. Ana-Alicia's (below) character, Melissa Agretti, was sometimes friend, sometimes foe.

Falcon Crest: A tense scene with Morgan Fairchild as Jordan Roberts.

Richard and Maggie.

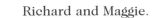

Selby as Xavier Trout in *Soldier of Fortune, Inc.* (renamed *SOF: Special Ops Force*) talks with his daughter.

Below: With Brad Johnson and Tim Abell.

Trout with team leader Matt Shephard (Brad Johnson).

Joining in combat on
Soldier of Fortune, Inc.

Enjoying a light moment on the set (below).

In 1970, Selby first played
Abraham Lincoln on television
in *The Flatboatman* presentation
on the ABC Sunday afternoon
drama program *Directions*.

Leslie Charleston and Selby in the
ABC Wide World of Mystery presentation
The Norming Of Jack 243.

Washington: Behind Closed Doors with Meg Foster as
Selby's girlfriend. Selby played an opportunistic C.P.A. named
Roger Castle in the 12-hour *ABC Novel for Television*.

Behind the scenes in
*Washington: Behind Closed
Doors*, with Jason Robards.

Telethon, with Eve Plumb (above left) and John Marley.

Selby with *The Night Rider* co-star Percy Rodriguez above and the townsfolk, including Harris Yulin, George Grizzard and Pernell Roberts.

The Night Rider:
Kim Cattrall played his sister.

Finally getting to be a swashbuckler in *The Night Rider*.

Patty Duke and Selby were husband and wife in *Grave Secrets: The Legacy of Hilltop Drive* (produced under the title of *The Black Hope Horror*).

No, it's not porno—
it's *Jackie Collins'
Lady Boss*.

Love for Rent with Lisa Eilbacher and Annette O'Toole.

In mini-series *King Of The Olympics: The Lives and Loves of Avery Brundage*, Selby played Brundage from young adult through old age.

Avery Brundage: the athlete.

Sybil Maas portrayed Brundage's wife, Elizabeth Dunlap.
Renée Soutendijk played his mistress, Linnea Dresden.

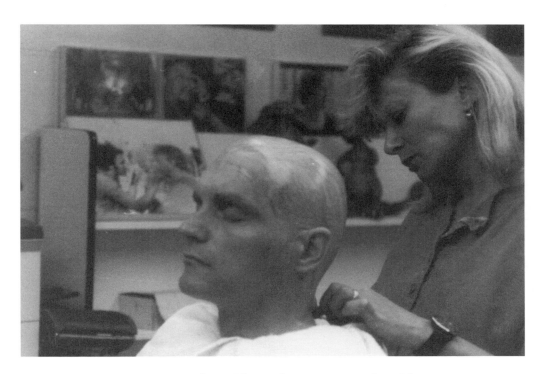

Aging Avery Brundage. The make-up artist is Dee Monsano.

Avery Brundage with his two
children by his mistress.

Brundage with Hitler during the '36 Olympics.

With Hume Cronyn in *Horton Foote's Alone.*

Guest starring on the CBS series *Promised Land*.

Selby played Abraham Lincoln on an episode of *Touched By An Angel*.

MY ALBUM

The faded indiginities
and indiscretions
mere youthful mortalities
An old curtain
stained with humility
covers the window
of old realities with new
pictures in my album
They are brighter
more composed
Every mundane incident
an occasion
focused and facinating
leading somewhere
I look at them
over and over
I have a cot
a wooden chair
a small table
a solitary light
and my album
nothing else
Every evening I bend
over my album and touch
each picture
going back
all the way
The voices are clearer
as are the apologies
the hearts are purer
the love is deeper
Not a picture is wasted
Thank you God
and thank you dear

DAVID SELBY CREDITS

DAYTIME TV

Series Regular:

Dark Shadows, Quentin Collins; 1968-71

Guest Appearances:

Directions, ("The Flatboatman")
Abraham Lincoln; 70

Dark Shadows

PRIMETIME TV

Series Regular:

Soldier of Fortune, Inc./Special Ops Force, Xavier Trout; 97-99
Falcon Crest, Richard Channing; 82-90
Flamingo Road, Michael Tyrone; 82

Guest Appearances:

Touched By An Angel, ("Beautiful Dreamer") Abraham Lincoln; 98
Promised Land, ("Cowboy Blues") Rowdy; 97
Family, ("More Than Friends") Michael Kagan; 78
Kojak, ("An Unfair Trade") James O'Connor; 76
Police Woman, ("No Place To Hide") Nate Fesler; 75
The Waltons ("The Romance") Joshua Williams; 74

*Soldier
of Fortune, Inc.*

TV MOVIES

Horton Foote's Alone, Paul; 97
Jackie Collins' Lady Boss, Martin Swanson; 92; mini-series
Grave Secrets: The Legacy of Hilltop Drive, Shag Williams; 92
King of the Olympics: The Lives and Loves of Avery Brundage,
    Avery Brundage; 88; mini-series

Doctor Franken, Dr. Mike Foster;
    80; pilot
Love for Rent, Phil; 79
The Night Rider, Lord Thomas
    Earl/Chalk Hollister; 79; pilot
Telethon, Roy Hansen; 77
Washington: Behind Closed Doors,
    Roger Castle; 77; mini-series
The Norming of Jack 243, Jack 243; 75

The Night Rider

FILM

Mighty Ducks 3, Dean Buckley; 96
White Squall, Francis Beaumont; 96
Headless Body in a Topless Bar, Bradford Lumkin; 95
Intersection, Richard Quarry; 94
Dying Young, aka *Choice of Love*, Richard Geddes; 91
Rich and Famous, Doug Blake; 81
Raise the Titanic, Dr. Gene Seagram; 80
Rich Kids, Steve Sloan; 79
Super Cops, Robert Hantz;
    73
The Girl in Blue aka *U-Turn*,
    Scott Laithan; 72
Up the Sandbox, Paul
    Reynolds; 72
Night of Dark Shadows,
    QuentinCollins/
    Charles Collins; 71

The Girl in Blue

STAGE

A Long Day's Journey Into Night, James Tyrone; 98; Houston, TX;
   99; Hartford, CT

Lincoln and James, Abraham Lincoln; 99; Washington, D.C.

The Perfectionist, Tobias Harte; 93;
   Princeton, NJ

A Lincoln Portrait, Narrator; 93;
   Morgantown, WV

Money and Friends, Stephen; 93;
   Los Angeles, CA

Much Ado About Nothing, Benedick;
   92; Washington, DC

Night of the Iguana, Rev. Lawrence
   Shannon; 91; Los Angeles, CA

The Crucible, John Proctor; 90;
   Los Angeles, CA

Love Letters, Andy; 90;
   Pasadena, CA

Sticks and Bones

Hedda Gabler, Eibert Lovberg; 81;
   Boston, MA & Stamford, CT

A Woman In Paris, 81; Garden City, NY

I Won't Dance, Dom; 80-81; Buffalo, NY & New York NY

The Rehearsal, The Count; 87; Los Angeles, CA

A Hundred Percent Alive (aka *The Slugger*), Dave Krelack;
   79; Los Angeles, CA

Back in the Race, 79; New York, NY

The Children's Hour, Dr. Joseph Cardin; 78; Stockbridge, MA

Toys in the Attic, Julian Berniers; 78; Princeton, NJ & Philadelphia, PA

Ribcage, Hodge; 78; West Springfield, MA & New York, NY

The Playboy of the Western World, Christy Mahon; 77; New York, NY

Eccentricities of a Nightingale, Dr. John Buchanan Jr.; 76; Buffalo, NY &
   New York, NY

The Heiress, Morris Townsend; 76; Washington, D.C. & New York, NY

The Family, Doc; 75; New York, NY

Cat on a Hot Tin Roof, Brick Pollick; 75; National Tour

Henry IV, Prince Hal; 74; Chicago, IL

Dance on a Country Grave, Clym Yeobright; 74; Arlington Park, IL

Echoes, Sam; 73; New York, NY

Siamese Connections, Franklin Kroner Jr.; 73; New York, NY

Sticks and Bones, David; 71-72; New York, NY

Gandhi, The Antagonist; 70; New York, NY

The Devil's Disciple, Dick Dudgeon; 70; Stratford, CT

The Unseen Hand, Cisco Morphan; 70; New York, NY

Forensic and the Navigator, Emmet; 70; New York, NY

Mr. High Pockets, Abraham Lincoln; 68; Carbondale, IL

Dear Charles, Walter; 68; Paramus, NJ

Yes, My Darling Daughter, Doug Hall; 68; New York, NY

For God and Country and Mrs. Corrine, Country; 67; New York, NY

The Impossible Years,
    David Merrick; 67; New
    York, NY & National Tour

The Tempest, Alonso;
    67; Cleveland, OH

Brecht on Brecht, various;
    66; Cleveland, OH

USA, various; 66;
    Cleveland, OH

The Hostage, 66;
    Cleveland, OH

You Never Can Tell,
    Mr. Valentine; 66;
    Abington, VA

The Crucible, 66;
    Abington, VA

Long Day's Journey Into Night.

You Can't Take It with You, Tony; 66; Abington, VA

Marat/Sade, 66; Abington, VA

Krapp's Last Tape, Krapp; 66; Abington, VA

The Cave Dwellers, Gorky; 66; Abington, VA

Fugitive Masks, The Manager; 66; Abington, VA

Inherit the Wind, Henry Drummond; 65; Carbondale, IL

Prologue to Glory, 65; Carbondale, IL

The Last Days of Lincoln, Abraham Lincoln; 65; Carbondale, IL

Oedipus Rex, Oedipus; 64; Carbondale, IL

Romeo and Juliet, Mercutio; 63; Morgantown, WV

Oklahoma, Will Parker; 62; Morgantown, WV

Tiger at the Gates, Hector; 61; Morgantown, WV

Brigadoon, Sandy Dean; 61; Morgantown, WV

Honey in the Rock, Rev. Butelle; 61; Beckley, WV

RADIO

National Public Radio dramatic presentations of classics with
L.A. Theatre Works, including:

> *The Rehearsal*, 89; *The Master and Margarita*, 91; *Heaven and
> Earth*, 91; *The Perfectionist*, 94; *McTeague*, 95; *State of the Union*, 96;
> *The Misanthrope*, 97; *Ruby McCollum*, 97; *Babbitt*, 98; *The Young Man
> From Atlanta*, 98; *A Streetcar Named Desire*, 98

MISCELLANEOUS (partial listing)

Where's Nova Scotia?, 98; staged reading of play written by David
West Virginia: A Film History, 95; documentary, voice only
The Shot, Gordon Sunshine; 93; New York University film short